Liberty A.I. Company

THE 19 SKYSCRAPERS MOST FAMOUS OF NEW YORK

The complete guide

The 19 MOST FAMOUS SKYSCRAPERS IN NEW YORK:
THE COMPLETE GUIDE

The work is the result of the author's research. It is forbidden to reproduce, even partially, without the consent of the author to whom all rights are entitled. ©

The 19 MOST FAMOUS SKYSCRAPERS IN NEW YORK:
THE COMPLETE GUIDE

Summary:

1. Empire State Building
2. One World Trade Center
3. The Chrysler Building
4. Bank of America Tower
5. The Woolworth Building
6. New York Times Building
7. 432 Park Avenue
8. Rockefeller Center
9. Trump Tower
10. Steinway Tower
11. 70 Pine Street
12. MetLife Building
13. Citigroup Center
14. 30 Hudson Yards
15. Time Warner Center
16. Spruce Street – Beekman Tower
17. The Helmsley Building
18. Central Park Tower
19. Flat Iron Building |

Empire State Building

The Empire State Building is one of New York's most iconic landmarks and one of the most famous skyscrapers in the world. Located at the intersection of Fifth Avenue and West 34th Street, the building was built during the Great Depression and has become a symbol of hope and progress for the entire nation.

The project was presented in 1929 by John J. Raskob, an American businessman who had made his fortune in the automotive field, convinced that the building could be a symbol of American power and success. He decided to entrust the design to the architect William F. Lamb of the architectural firm Shreve, Lamb and Harmon.

Its construction began in March 1930 and employed about 3,400 workers.

The skyscraper was completed in just 410 days, a real record for the time, and inaugurated on May 1, 1931, although the finishing and interior decoration works lasted for a few more months.

The Empire State Building is 1,454 feet (443.2 meters) tall to the top of the antenna, has 85 elevators and 6,500 windows. At its opening, it was the tallest building in the world, surpassing the record held by the Chrysler Building.

It was built to be the headquarters of Raskob's company, General Motors. However, due to the Great Depression of 1929, the G.M. decided not to move into the building and the property had to look for other tenants.

In the 50s and 60s, the building underwent a number of changes, including the addition of an antenna for television broadcasting.

In the 80s, it was the subject of a series of acquisitions by several companies, including the Donald Trump Organization, which attempted to buy the building in full, but was rejected by the owner of the time, Helmsley-Spear.

In 2006, the Empire State Building was acquired by a consortium of investors led by real estate management company Malkin Holdings, which initiated a major program of renovation and modernization of the building.

Today, it is one of New York City's most popular tourist attractions, with over four million visitors a year. The building houses offices and shops, but the real highlight is the observatory, located on the 86th floor, which offers spectacular panoramic views of the city.

It was designed in the Art Deco style, the dominant art and design movement in the 20s and 30s. The exterior of the building has many of the typical features of this style, such as geometric lines, square shapes and metal decorations. In addition, the tower features a number of details and ornaments, such as relief cornices, columns, and floral details that distinguish it from other skyscrapers.

One of the most iconic features is its stepped crown at the top. This element was added after the designers decided to increase the height of the building to overcome the Chrysler Building.

The interiors have also been designed with care and attention. The atrium is decorated with marble and fine wood. The walls with mosaics representing scenes of work and everyday life.

Over 60,000 tons of structural steel, 200,000 square meters of glass, 10 million bricks and 730 tons of aluminum were used for the construction of the skyscraper.

Its implementation was divided into five phases. The first consisted in the construction of the foundations that were dug to a depth of 22 meters below street level. The second in the installation of the steel columns, while the third phase involved the installation of horizontal beams to create the floors of the building. The fourth phase consisted of laying the steel plates and concrete for the creation of the façade of the building, while the fifth and final phase involved the installation of the elevators, the heating system and the electrical system.

The construction of the Empire State Building was made possible thanks to the use of innovative technologies for the time. For example, workers used crane bridges and suspended work platforms to move along the structure.

The use of steel as the main material made it possible to create a lightweight and durable skeleton.

The Empire State Building was officially opened on May 1, 1931 in a ceremony attended by numerous representatives of the political and cultural world. On that occasion, the president of the United States at the time, Herbert Hoover, connected the skyscraper to the national telephone network through a call made from the White House.

Over the years there have been several maintenance and renovations necessary to ensure its safety and energy efficiency.

In the 50s, fire protection was added to the corridors, while in the 60s the old elevators were replaced with new, faster and more efficient models. In the 80s, the Empire State Building underwent a complete renovation of the heating, ventilation and air conditioning system, which significantly reduced energy consumption and saved millions of dollars in bills.

In the 2000s, the skyscraper underwent a major renovation, aimed at improving its energy efficiency and making it more environmentally sustainable. The old windows were replaced with new high-efficiency models, heat recovery systems and photovoltaic systems for the production of solar energy were installed.

The Empire State Building is a skyscraper for mainly commercial use, and is divided into various spaces for offices and commercial activities. The ground floor houses the large entrance hall where there are some commercial activities and access to the various elevators leading to the upper floors.

Floors 1 to 20 are mainly intended for offices, with a wide range of companies occupying the spaces. Some of these are also accessible to the public. It also has a range of on-site facilities, including a large dining area, conference rooms and a gym. In all, the skyscraper covers an area of about 257,000 square meters.

Throughout its history, the building has seen some tragic accidents. The most serious occurred on July 28, 1945, when a B-25 Mitchell military aircraft crashed into the north side hitting the 79th floor. The accident caused the death of 14 people on board the plane and 11 others inside the skyscraper. The impact caused a huge fire, which destroyed several floors. A fire in 1962 caused damage to the 66th floor.

Currently, the Empire State Building is owned by the Empire State Realty Trust, a public real estate company that owns and operates several commercial buildings in New York City. The company acquired it in 2013.

The building houses a wide variety of renters, including businesses, nonprofits, television and film production studios, and special event spaces. Among the best known are:

- Global advertising agency IPG Mediabrands.

- The telecommunications and internet company Verizon Communications

- The Foot Locker chain of sporting goods stores.

- The Bluefly luxury e-commerce website.

- The ABC television network.

- The legendary radio station WNBC.

- The Foundation of the United Nations.

- The Human Rights Commission of the City of New York.

The Empire State Building is open to the public and offers various options for visiting the skyscraper and its observatory on the 86th floor, which offers breathtaking panoramic views of New York City.

There are several ways to buy tickets for the Empire State Building:

- online on the official website of the Empire State Building. This method of purchase allows you to avoid the long lines to buy tickets on the spot.

- on site directly at the Empire State Building, but you may have to wait in line to buy tickets.

- CityPASS which includes admission to the Empire State Building and other tourist attractions in the city at a discounted price.
- New York Pass which offers free admission to the Empire State Building and other New York City tourist attractions at a fixed price.

The Empire State Building is open 365 days a year, from 8:00 a.m. to 2:00 a.m. The entrance to the observatory on the 86th floor is located on Fifth Avenue, on the east side of the building. During peak tourist season, there may be long lines to access the Empire State Building. To avoid them it is advisable to go there early in the morning or after 20:00.

One World Trade Center

The One World Trade Center, also known as Freedom Tower, is a skyscraper located in Lower Manhattan. At 541 meters high, it is the tallest skyscraper in the United States and the Western Hemisphere.

The project was carried out by David Childs of Skidmore, Owings & Merrill. The design is based on a rectangular parallelepiped shape, with rounded corners and a spire of glass and stainless steel that rises upwards. It was built to replace the Twin Towers, destroyed in the attacks of September 11, 2001.

Construction began in 2006 and ended in 2013, at an estimated cost of approximately $3.9 billion. Several issues and delays occurred during the work, including an impasse between real estate developers Larry Silverstein and the Port Authority of New York and New Jersey.

The skyscraper was built using a wide range of materials, including reinforced concrete, stainless steel, glass and aluminum.

The exterior façade is characterized by a system of energy-efficient windows that filter sunlight and reduce heat. In addition, the skyscraper was designed to withstand earthquakes, hurricanes and fires.

At the top of the skyscraper is One World Observatory, a viewing platform that offers 360-degree views of New York City. It is accessible via high-speed elevators that take visitors to the top in seconds.

One World Trade Center quickly became an icon of New York City and the United States, a symbol of American resilience and determination after the attacks of September 11, 2001. It has become a popular tourist attraction, with millions of visitors each year coming to its summit to admire the views of the city.

The project was entrusted to the architectural firm Skidmore, Owings & Merrill (SOM), which won the international design competition. The design of One World Trade Center was led by architect David

Childs, who worked in collaboration with structural designer Leslie Robertson.

It initially featured a 1,776-foot-tall tower, in homage to the American Independence Year. However, this design was later modified for safety reasons and the tower was reduced to 1,368 feet.

The project required many years of planning and approval by local and federal authorities, along with important security considerations following the September 11 attacks.

The construction was financed with public and private funds, including a $1.2 billion loan from the U.S. government.

The building has a perfect parallelepiped shape with a series of diagonal cuts on its façade, which shrink as they get closer to the top. These cuts have been designed to increase the building's resistance to winds and to reflect sunlight dynamically, creating a striking visual effect.

Its design was influenced by the site where it is located and was driven by the need to create a building that respected its historical and symbolic importance.

It was built with a high-strength carbon steel frame and a reinforced concrete skeleton so as to withstand the weather, explosions and impacts of aircraft. The external cladding consists of an extensive window, which allows you to enjoy a panoramic view of the city.

The skyscraper was also built with recyclable materials in order to reduce the environmental impact of the construction and is equipped with a rainwater collection system, which is used for cooling and heating the interiors.

Its construction was not without its challenges and difficulties. The main problem that arose during construction was that of safety. After the attacks of September 11, 2001, the World Trade Center was considered a priority target for international terrorism.

To address this problem, some unprecedented measures had to be taken. First of all, the structure was designed to withstand terrorist attacks, with external boundary walls able to withstand explosions.

Another problem that arose was that of soil stability. The area around the construction site was known for its geological instability, which made it difficult to build the foundation. A system of steel poles driven into the ground was used.

One World Trade Center opened on November 3, 2014 and opened to the public on May 29, 2015. The ceremony was held in the presence of many authorities and families of the victims of the attacks of 11 September 2001. Guests in attendance included President Barack Obama, New York Governor Andrew Cuomo and New York Mayor Bill de Blasio.

The building has a total area of approximately 325,000 square meters. It has a main lobby and covers an area of approximately 9,000 square meters. It is accessible from the outside through several doors and has a large atrium, which creates a cozy and bright atmosphere thanks to the abundance of light.

The current owner is the US real estate company The Durst Organization which acquired a stake in 2010, following which it helped finance its construction. In 2013, the company came to 90% ownership.

The U.S. federal government also holds an interest in One World Trade Center through the General Services Administration (GSA), which has signed a long-term lease for several floors of the building to house the offices of federal agencies such as the FBI and the Internal Revenue Service (IRS).

There are numerous renters, including businesses, nonprofits, and government agencies. Some of the major renters include:

- Conde Nast: a major publishing house that publishes famous magazines such as Vogue, Vanity Fair, GQ and The New Yorker. Conde Nast was the first tenant to move into the tower, occupying 24 floors of the building.

- United States Immigration and Naturalization Service (USCIS): a government agency that deals with immigration issues. USCIS is located on several floors of the building.

- KidZania: an educational theme park for children, occupying several floors of the building.

- Legends Hospitality: a sports event management company that operates the "One World Observatory", the observatory located on the 102nd floor of the building.

- Global Citizen: a non-profit organization that deals with global issues such as poverty, climate change and social justice. Global Citizen is based on several floors of the building.

- GroupM: a media and marketing company that occupies several floors of the building.

- Beijing Vantone: a Chinese real estate investment company that bought an entire wing of the building to house its operations in the United States.

- BMB Group: an asset management and investment company that purchased space in One World Trade Center to house its American headquarters.

In addition to these renters, One World Trade Center also houses several restaurants, shops, banks, and other services to the public.

The skyscraper is open to the public for guided tours. The main observation deck of the building is called One World Observatory. It was opened to the public in 2015 and has become one of New York's top tourist attractions.

There are three ticket options available:

- Standard Experience: This ticket gives you access to the main observatory on the hundredth floor. You can enjoy a 360-degree panoramic view of the city, as well as an interactive exhibition about the building and New York City.

- Priority Experience: With this ticket, you get the fastest access to the observatory and a guided audio tour to discover the secrets of the building.

- All-Inclusive Experience: This ticket offers access to the observatory, a guided audio tour, breakfast or lunch at One Dine restaurant, and a souvenir of the building.

In addition, there are also special packages for events such as weddings, birthday parties and other celebrations.

To visit the observatory, you must book in advance on the official website of One World Observatory or through other services. You can also buy tickets at the observatory ticket office, but it is advisable to book in advance to avoid queues and waits.

Once at the building, visitors must pass through airport-like security and board a high-speed elevator that arrives at the observatory in seconds. The panoramic view of the city and its surroundings is truly spectacular and unforgettable.

The 19 MOST FAMOUS SKYSCRAPERS IN NEW YORK:
THE COMPLETE GUIDE

The Chrysler Building

The Chrysler Building is one of the most iconic skyscrapers in New York City and was for a few months the tallest in the world. Built in 1930, it was named in honor of automotive tycoon Walter Chrysler, who financed its construction.

The building is located at 405 Lexington Avenue, on the corner of 42nd Street, in the Midtown Manhattan neighborhood. Its construction was financed by the Chrysler Corporation, which intended to use it as the headquarters of their business.

The skyscraper is the result of the rivalry between Walter Chrysler and architect William H. Reynolds, who was designing the headquarters for the Bank of Manhattan. Chrysler wanted a building even taller than Reynolds, so they hired architect William Van Alen.

The final design was influenced by the

Art Deco style, characterized by geometric shapes, curved lines and ornamental details. The building has an elegant stainless steel façade, which gives it a distinctive appearance.

It is 319 meters high and has a dome-shaped turret of 38 meters, originally designed to be an antenna, but realized as an aesthetic element.

Its construction presented some challenges. Most of the steel was installed without the use of cranes, which could not reach the height of the building. Workers used a system of ropes and hoists to lift the sheets and beams.

Van Alen's project envisaged a skyscraper that would exceed in height the other buildings in the city. The design featured a horseshoe-shaped tower and a large conical arch, which would become its symbol. He was chosen from over ten proposals thanks to his originality and audacity.

Construction began in 1929 and was completed in just 18 months, a record time for the time. All the work was financed by Chrysler itself, which invested 20 million dollars.

The design had been kept secret until

the end of construction, when the tower was revealed to the public in May 1930.

The outer cladding is made of red brick and stainless steel, which blend harmoniously together. But the most iconic element of the Chrysler Building is its spire. Covered in stainless steel, it has numerous decorations, including six pinnacles that seem to stretch towards the sky. At the top is a lighthouse, which was originally intended to serve as a watchtower for ships entering New York Harbor.

A unique feature in the construction of the skyscraper was the use of the prefabrication system, which made it possible to reduce the construction time.

In total, the building required the production of approximately 3,826,000 bricks, 29,961 tons of steel and 3,826 glass panels.

During its construction there were several construction problems that slowed down the work. The first was the lack of funds, since the original budget had already been exceeded in the first months of construction. In addition, construction of the building began shortly after the Great Depression of 1929, which decreased the number of investors interested in financing the building.

Another problem was the location: the area was densely populated and vehicular traffic particularly intense. This made it difficult to deliver materials and manage the construction site. In addition, during construction, workers faced challenges related to heights, wind and adverse weather conditions. Several safety measures were taken, including the use of safety nets and the installation of bulkheads to protect workers.

Despite these problems, the construction of the Chrysler Building was completed in just 18 months of work and its inauguration took place on May 27, 1930, in the presence of the President of the United States of America at the time, Herbert Hoover.

The ceremony was a success and attracted a lot of attention. The building was immediately acclaimed as an architectural masterpiece and the largest skyscraper in the world, a title it held for only eleven months, until the construction of the Empire State Building. On the day of the inauguration, the skyscraper was illuminated by a system composed of 3,826 incandescent bulbs.

Over the years, the Chrysler Building has undergone several maintenance and renovations to preserve its original appearance and improve its functionality.

In 1967, the Cooper Union Foundation purchased the building for $18 million and began a complete renovation of the heating, cooling, and ventilation system, as well as upgrading the elevators. In 1978, the building was sold to Tishman Speyer Properties for $140 million.

In 1998, the stainless steel façade was cleaned and restored, removing stains and restoring the original appearance.

Over the years there have been some events that have affected the skyscraper. In 1945, a B-25 Mitchell military aircraft crashed into the skyscraper due to thick fog, killing 14 people on board the plane and one person inside the building.

In the 70s and 80s, there were some disputes regarding the ownership and management of the building. In 1978, the building's co-owner, real estate magnate Sol Atlas, attempted to sell his share to another company, but the decision was challenged in court by Atlas' sister, who claimed to have rights to the property. In 1981, control of the building passed to Cooper Union, a New York City school of art and design.

Although the Chrysler Building was designed to house primarily offices, the building has modular interior spaces, which can be divided and grouped for different uses. The ground floor houses a large atrium with vaulted ceiling, marble floors and stone walls. This space is accessible to the public. The lobby has been decorated with mosaics and metal reliefs, depicting humanity's advances in technology, science and industry.

The upper floors house offices of various sizes, from small suites to large open spaces. Each floor has bathrooms and a coffee break. The interior spaces have been designed to be functional, but also comfortable and elegant. The floor-to-ceiling windows offer spectacular views of New York City.

As many as 32 elevators serve the 77 floors of the building.

The Chrysler Building is currently owned by RFR Holding LLC, founded by Aby Rosen and Michael Fuchs. The company acquired the building in 1998 for $210 million. Prior to RFR Holding, the Chrysler Building passed through several proprietary hands and was also the subject of an initial public offering in 1969. However, public ownership did not last long, and in 1979 Cooper Union, a New York educational institution, acquired the building for $60 million.

In 1997, Tishman Speyer Properties acquired the Chrysler Building from Cooper Union for $220 million before RFR Holding LLC acquired it the following year.

Among the main tenants of the skyscraper are companies such as Japanese bank DKB, Springer publishing house Science+Business Media, human resources consulting firm Allegis Group, investment firm Abu Dhabi Investment Council and financial advisory firm FTI Consulting. In addition, the ground floor houses several retail stores, including a tourist gadget shop, a sweet shop, and a beauty salon.

In the past, the Chrysler Building has also been leased to other major companies and institutions, including American Airlines, the Associated Press news agency, toy maker Hasbro and NYU Langone Medical Center.

Being a private building it is not open to the public for sightseeing. However, the building's interiors are accessible during office hours for renters and authorized visitors. The main entrances are located on 42nd Street and Lexington Avenue.

Art Deco elevators take you to the various floors of the building, but a permit is required to access the upper floors.

The dome of the building is not open

to the public, but you can admire it from the street. The Chrysler Building was designed to be seen from below and to admire its architectural beauty from the outside.

Bank of America Tower

The Bank of America Tower is a skyscraper located in New York, in the Midtown Manhattan neighborhood, which rises to 366 meters and has 55 floors. It was designed by Cook + Fox Architects, who chose to build it using sustainable materials and cutting-edge technologies. Its construction began in 2004 and ended in 2009.

The design is modern and innovative. The tower is characterized by a glass façade, which reflects the sky and the surrounding skyscrapers. The shape is slender, with a series of curves that give it a dynamic appearance.

It was built using sustainable materials, such as recycled steel, low-carbon concrete and FSC-certified wood. The façade consists of a double layer of glass, which allows to reduce the greenhouse effect and to limit the use of air conditioning.

His project began in 2004, when the Bank of America acquired a 4,200-square-foot plot of land in the heart of Manhattan's financial district with the goal of creating a sustainable, energy-efficient building that met the highest standards. The design therefore had a strong impact on the choice of materials and technologies used.

The Bank of America Tower was the first skyscraper in New York to achieve LEED (Leadership in Energy and Environmental Design) Platinum certification, the highest level of environmental certification in the United States.

The work underwent a series of changes during the construction phase and the total estimated cost was 1 billion dollars.

The design presents a modern and minimalist aesthetic, characterized by clean lines and open spaces. The building was designed with a series of curves that create an elongated V-shape.

One of the distinctive features is its "aeropulitura" system, which uses a method of mechanical openings to regulate ventilation in the building and reduce energy consumption. Inside, the focus on sustainable design and the health and well-being of the occupants is evident in all aspects. There are hanging gardens and terraces.

The tower was officially opened on May 1, 2009, although parts of the building had been opened to the public before that date. The ceremony was chaired by New York City Mayor Michael Bloomberg, Bank of America CEO Ken Lewis and many other representatives of the institutions and companies involved in the construction. It represented a moment of great pride for the city of New York and for the entire country, as the building was designed and built with the aim of achieving a high level of environmental sustainability, becoming one of the most ecological skyscrapers in the world.

The building has undergone several maintenance operations in the years following its inauguration.

In 2014, solar panels were installed on the roof to increase renewable energy production. In 2015, renovations were completed on the atrium, which received a new marble floor, new walls and ceilings, as well as a new lighting system. In 2016, new smart elevators were installed, which can reduce waiting times.

The interior spaces are divided to

accommodate offices, shops and other commercial activities. The ground floor is a large area that serves as an exhibition space and houses a number of restaurants. The upper floors are reserved for offices and host many international and national companies. There are: Bank of America, financial advisory firm Guggenheim Partners, insurance company AIG, consulting firm Deloitte and many others.

The building also has a dedicated conference and meeting area. The main one is located on the 54th floor.

The tower is owned by the Durst Organization, a New York real estate company, and Bank of America, which owns a portion of it.

The Bank of America Tower is not open to the public for sightseeing, as it is primarily a commercial building. However, there are some parts of the building that are accessible such as the shops on the ground floor.

The Woolworth Building

The Woolworth Building is a historic skyscraper designed by architect Cass Gilbert and built between 1910 and 1913. It was the tallest skyscraper in the world until 1930, with its 241 meters high and 57 floors.

The project was commissioned by Frank W. Woolworth, founder of the Woolworth department store chain and involved the construction of a building that would house the company's offices, as well as commercial and catering spaces.

The art and design of the Woolworth Building reflects the neo-Gothic style of the era, with elaborate architectural details and widespread use of materials such as marble and bronze. The façade of the skyscraper is decorated with sculptures, gargoyles and mullioned windows, while inside there are frescoes and mosaics.

It was built using a steel structure, with a terracotta façade. The pyramid roof is made of copper.

The project was born from the desire of Frank Winfield Woolworth to build his headquarters in New York. He contacted the architect Cass Gilbert and entrusted him with the task of creating a skyscraper that was "as tall as possible". Cass Gilbert was inspired by Rouen Cathedral in France.

The project was approved and work began in 1910 with an initial budget of $5 million.

During its construction, numerous other materials were also used, such as granite, marble for the stairs and floor of the ground floor and bronze for the doors and windows. The building was the first in the world to be equipped with high-speed elevators, made by the Otis Elevator Company.

The construction of the Woolworth Building was not without its difficulties. One of the main problems was the location of the construction site near the metro.

In addition, the skyscraper was built on swampy and muddy ground, making it necessary to use a series of reinforced concrete poles to create a platform for the building.

It was inaugurated on April 24, 1913

with an official ceremony attended by political and business personalities.

Despite being designed as an office skyscraper, its wide base allowed the presence of some shops. The ground floor was built to be a large commercial area with large windows overlooking the street.

The Woolworth Building was also designed with spaces for private life, as Frank Woolworth intended to use some of the upper floors as his personal residence. The 29th floor was a private luxury apartment with nine rooms, a large living room, a dining room, a solarium, a library and a cinema room.

Today, the Woolworth Building has been converted into a mix of office space and private residences. The first occupy the lower floors, while the private residences are located from floors 29 to 58.

Currently, the building is owned by the Witkoff Group, an American real estate company. Renters include several companies: consulting firm PwC, marketing agency Sailthru, investment firm Silverstein Properties, Woolworth Historical Archive Foundation and many others.

The Woolworth Building is not open to the public for sightseeing. However, you can admire the exterior from the street. During the Christmas period, the building is particularly impressive thanks to the bright decorations that adorn it.

The 19 MOST FAMOUS SKYSCRAPERS IN NEW YORK:
THE COMPLETE GUIDE

The New York Times Building

The New York Times Building is a skyscraper located in the Times Square area of Manhattan. Opened in 2007, it was designed by Italian architect Renzo Piano in collaboration with architecture group FXFOWLE.

It has a structure of 52 floors and reaches a height of 319 meters. It was built with the aim of obtaining LEED (Leadership in Energy and Environmental Design) certification, which means that it has a special focus on energy efficiency and environmental sustainability.

The project was conceived with the aim of creating a modern and innovative workspace for the editorial staff of the New York Times.

The exterior of the skyscraper is characterized by a modern and clean design, with a glass façade that reflects the surrounding skyline. The parallelepiped shape is broken by a series of vertical cuts, which create a sort of "veins".

The New York Times Building project was first unveiled in 2000, when the newspaper of the same name announced plans to build a new headquarters. The building was supposed to replace the previous one located in an unsafe and unattractive place.

The proposed design was based on a number of key concepts, including transparency, sustainability and interactivity. It involved the use of advanced materials and technologies to minimize environmental impact.

The exterior of the building is characterized by a double-skin façade consisting of a cladding of glass panels that extends throughout the height of the building, alternating with vertical bands of stainless steel. The skyscraper develops in height with a diamond-shaped cross section.

A distinctive feature of the exterior of The New York Times Building is the presence of a large LED screen that extends the entire width of the building's south façade. It broadcasts real-time news and traffic and weather related information.

The building is equipped with a roof

garden that serves as a green area for employees and as a rainwater collection system.

The construction of The New York Times Building presented some significant challenges. One of the main problems the engineers faced was designing a structure that could withstand the strong gusts of wind that occur in that area.

Inaugurated on November 19, 2007, it was open to the public from the next day, November 20. The ceremony was chaired by New York City Mayor Michael Bloomberg, New York Times Company Chairman of the Board of Directors Arthur Sulzberger Jr. and Chairman and Chief Executive Officer Janet Robinson.

The interior spaces are divided into several sections, including offices, conference rooms, press rooms and common areas. The building has been LEED (Leadership in Energy and Environmental Design) certified for its energy efficiency and sustainability.

The New York Times Building is owned by the New York Times Company and primarily houses the editorial office of the New York Times. However, part of the space is rented to other companies, including software company Microsoft, advertising agency Droga5 and financial services company ING.

Apart from the entrance area, the lobby and some food services, the building is not open to the public as it is a complex for the exclusive use of the editorial staff of The New York Times and other companies based there.

Il 432 Park Avenue

The 432 Park Avenue is a skyscraper of 96 floors and 426 meters high located in Midtown Manhattan. Its minimalist and smooth design was designed by Uruguayan architect Rafael Viñoly. The property was completed in 2015.

The line is characterized by straight profiles and a cubic shape, with floor-to-ceiling windows. The façade is clad in white Tennessee marble. Its structure consists of a series of reinforced concrete pillars.

The skyscraper has 12 private elevators and a computerized heating and cooling system.

It has 104 apartments. Each with an area of 500 to 1,400 square meters, for a total of 46,000 square meters of living space.

The interiors are designed by interior design studio Deborah Berke Partners and feature luxurious finishes. It features a wide range of facilities including a gym, swimming pool, spa, conference room, children's area and private parking.

The project was born in 2006, when the real estate developer Macklowe Properties bought the Drake Hotel building for 440 million dollars with the idea of demolishing it and building a new luxury residential skyscraper. Rafael Viñoly presented the design in 2011.

The design is characterized by a very slender rectangular shape and with a series of square windows that extend from floor to ceiling. The project was received with great enthusiasm by the public and the media. Construction of the building began in 2012 and ended in 2015, at a total cost of approximately $1.25 billion.

The design of 432 Park Avenue was inspired by the simplicity and elegance of modernism, emphasizing the verticality of the skyscraper. The body consists of a single central column, surrounded by floor-to-ceiling windows, which reflect sunlight.

In terms of architectural style, the tower has been called "neo-rationalist", a fusion between the Italian rationalism of the 30s and the American modernism of the 60s. Its simple, linear shape stands out from other Manhattan skyscrapers.

During its construction there were some realization problems. The project has been the subject of much criticism regarding the environmental impact and the possible alteration of the urban profile of New York. In addition, the proximity to other skyscrapers and its height posed a technical challenge for the builders.

In addition, the building, which rises to 426 meters, was built in an area exposed to the winds. To mitigate this problem, engineers had to use special steel for the structure and draw lines with aerodynamic shapes.

Another problem was that of the foundation. Since the building is very tall and heavy, the foundations had to be particularly solid and deep.

Finally, the project encountered some difficulties from a regulatory point of view. Some restrictions on skyscrapers were imposed after the attacks of September 11, 2001, which involved a series of permits and permits to proceed with construction. But despite these problems, the construction of the building was completed in 2015.

432 Park Avenue opened on November 10, 2015, although the first housing units were completed and sold by

2013. The official ceremony was attended by many prominent personalities, including architect Rafael Viñoly and project co-developer Harry B. Macklowe.

The building has garnered great attention from both the media and the public, in part because of its imposing height and its dominant presence in Manhattan's urban landscape. The inauguration therefore represented an important milestone for the project and attracted many visitors.

The main entrance is located on Park Avenue and leads to an elegant and spacious lobby from which you can access the common facilities.

Apartments feature minimalist, modern architecture, with upscale finishes like bleached oak floors, Italian marble, and American walnut wood cabinets. Each residence has a panoramic view of New York thanks to the large floor-to-ceiling windows.

Access to the apartments is possible through private elevators that lead directly to the house.

432 Park Avenue is owned by CIM Group and Macklowe Properties, with Harry Macklowe as main owner. However, most of the 96 luxury apartments were sold to individuals or real estate companies. Among

the well-known owners are several billionaires and celebrities, such as Brazilian real estate mogul Alexandre Grendene Bartelle, Utah Jazz basketball team owner Ryan Smith, former Marvel Entertainment CEO Isaac Perlmutter, and singer Jennifer Lopez. Some apartments are also available for short-term rental via home-sharing services like Airbnb.

Access to the skyscraper is restricted to residents and their authorized guests.

The 19 MOST FAMOUS SKYSCRAPERS IN NEW YORK:
THE COMPLETE GUIDE

The 19 MOST FAMOUS SKYSCRAPERS IN NEW YORK:
THE COMPLETE GUIDE

Rockefeller Center

The Rockefeller Center is a complex of 19 buildings located in the Midtown Manhattan neighborhood of New York City. It was built by the Rockefeller family in the 30s of the twentieth century and still today represents one of the most important and iconic architectural complexes of the city. Its construction began in 1930 and ended in 1939.

It was designed by the architect Raymond Hood, who conceived a work of great artistic and cultural importance. It blends perfectly with the surrounding urban fabric. The aesthetic was influenced by the stylistic choices of the period.

The complex features an Art Deco design, characterized by clean lines and luxurious materials. It looks like a series of towers and low buildings with large green spaces and inner courtyards.

The project was born in the '20s, when the oil magnate John D. Rockefeller decided to invest in a real estate complex that could redevelop the Midtown Manhattan area north of Grand Central Station.

The tycoon contacted architect Raymond Hood and sculptor Lee Lawrie. Work began in 1931 and lasted for 9 years, until 1939, when the structure was inaugurated. During construction, efforts were made to employ as many local workers as possible, due to the Great Depression that had hit the United States.

The design and style were inspired by the architectural trends of the time, in particular by Art Deco, an artistic and architectural movement that had great success in the 20s and 30s. This style was characterized by the use of precious materials such as marble, bronze and glass as well as attention to decorative details and symmetry of forms.

Its construction was complicated due to the vast extension of the real estate complex. One of the main problems was the financing of the project, supported by John D. Rockefeller Jr. himself with the contribution of other major investors.

But during its construction there were some problems of realization. The base on which the buildings would rise consisted of a very hard rock mass that required a great deal of effort to remove.

In addition, the construction of the towers was very complicated from an engineering point of view, with the need to use cranes to lift the materials. But despite these problems, the project was carried out thanks to Rockefeller's commitment and the expertise of his collaborators, including the group of architects led by Raymond Hood and Wallace Harrison.

It was officially opened on May 1, 1933, during the Great Depression. The event was accompanied by a grand ceremony attended by President Franklin D. Roosevelt.

The buildings that make up the complex are arranged to form a central courtyard, known as "The Channel Gardens" where there is a golden statue of the Greek God Apollo

The most well-known building is "30 Rockefeller Plaza", commonly known as "30 Rock". The building has a "U" shape and extends over 70 floors. Other important buildings are: the "Comcast Building" (also known as "30 Rockefeller Plaza West"), the

"Time-Life Building", the "Radio City Music Hall" and the "Rainbow Room".

The interior spaces are designed to house offices, television studios, retail stores and restaurants. Most of the buildings are accessible to the public and there are numerous tourist attractions inside including the "Top of the Rock Observation Deck", which offers panoramic views of the city.

Rockefeller Center is owned by Rockefeller Group, a real estate company of the well-known American family. Currently, most of the space is leased to corporations and organizations, including NBCUniversal, Bank of America, Deloitte, Time Inc., and many others.

The complex offers numerous activities and attractions for visitors, including:

Top of the Rock - a rooftop terrace located on top of the GE Building, from which you can admire panoramic views of New York City, including the surrounding skyscrapers such as the Empire State Building and the Freedom Tower. It is open daily from 8:00 to 24:00.

Radio City Music Hall - an iconic concert hall where shows and concerts are organized throughout the year.

NBC Studios Tour - a guided tour that allows visitors to visit NBC television studios and learn how television programs are produced.

The Rink at Rockefeller Center - an outdoor ice skating rink, open during the winter season.

To visit the complex, visitors can reach the site via public transportation, including the metro and buses. You can book tickets to attractions online to avoid long queues.

The 19 MOST FAMOUS SKYSCRAPERS IN NEW YORK:
THE COMPLETE GUIDE

The 19 MOST FAMOUS SKYSCRAPERS IN NEW YORK:
THE COMPLETE GUIDE

Trump Tower

The Trump Tower is a residential and commercial skyscraper located at 725 Fifth Avenue on the southeast corner of 56th Street in Manhattan. It was designed by architect Der Scutt and built by real estate magnate Donald Trump in collaboration with the Equitable Life Assurance Society.

Construction began in 1979 and was completed in 1983. The building is 202 meters high, has 58 floors and 203 residential units, a postmodernist architectural style that presents art-deco and neoclassical elements.

The exterior features a glass and steel façade that rises on a pink and black granite plinth, with a large double-height entrance and a sign that reads "TRUMP" in golden letters.

Inside the building, the first six floors are reserved for shops, restaurants and offices, while the upper floors house luxury residences.

It also has a number of works of art, including a 6-meter-high bronze fountain, "The Universe," created by sculptor Joaquín Vaquero Turcios, which is located in the center of the tower's large atrium.

Trump Tower has been the center of public attention for several reasons, including its association with Donald Trump.

The project was conceived in 1979 by Donald Trump in collaboration with the architect Der Scutt. The building was built on a plot of land located at the intersection of Fifth Avenue and 56th Street in the heart of Manhattan.

The idea was to create a luxury residential complex that would offer spectacular views of New York City. Trump and Scutt worked closely together to define the appearance and layout. In the end, they opted for a parallelepiped-shaped structure 58 stories high.

It was built using 2,000 tons of steel and 70,000 square meters of glass.

The Trump Tower project met with criticism from the architectural community, who considered it too tall and unsuitable for the area. However, the building was a great success among buyers of luxury real estate.

The construction was subject to

several problems during the realization. One of the main ones was to buy the land necessary for construction, already occupied by shops and restaurants. Trump had to negotiate with landlords and in some cases had to use legal force to obtain property. In addition, its construction caused controversy regarding the demolition of the famous Bonwit Teller Building, a historic building in New York. The ground floor of the skyscraper is occupied by luxury shops and restaurants, while the first floor houses a large conference room and some meeting rooms. The second floor is the hotel area, which includes the reception, lounge and cafeteria. The 30th floor houses a luxury gym of 600 square meters with state-of-the-art equipment, sauna, massage room. Further up is Donald Trump's private residence, with a panoramic view of New York.Trump Tower is open to the public and can be visited free of charge. However, some parts of the building, such as residential apartments and offices, are only accessible to those who have permission.

You can access from the main entrance located on 5th Avenue, where there is a large lobby with precious marbles, crystal chandeliers and a large decorative waterfall.

111 West 57th Street - Steinway Tower

The skyscraper 111 West 57th Street, also known as the Steinway Tower, is a luxury residential building located in the Midtown neighborhood of Manhattan. The skyscraper, 435 meters high, was designed by the architectural firm JDS Development Group and the architectural firm SHoP Architects and was completed in 2019.

The building's site is within walking distance of Central Park and Manhattan's famous 57th Street, one of the city's most prestigious streets.

Its design has a slender and thin shape, with a glass façade. The skyscraper stands with a slender but durable structure that seems to defy gravity. It has a slender shape, with a section of only 17 meters wide, which makes it one of the thinnest towers in the world. It was built using advanced technologies, including a system of steel cables that connects the building to the underlying rock.

The skyscraper was designed to hold 46 luxury apartments, including some of the largest and most expensive in the world.

Residences vary in size: from the smallest units of 130 square meters to the largest ones of more than 650 square meters and include luxury finishes such as European oak floors, marble bathrooms, high-end appliances, and custom heating and cooling systems.

The construction of 111 West 57th Street had some construction problems. One of the main ones was that of proximity to underground metro lines.

To ensure stability it was necessary to opt for an innovative foundation technology with the use of steel pillars that penetrate the ground to a depth of 70 meters.

The tower was inaugurated in 2021, after seven years of work. The ceremony was celebrated with a party attended by many personalities from the real estate and fashion world.

The skyscraper is not open to the public for visits. Access is strictly limited to residents and their guests. But its design can be admired from the outside by walking down 57th Street.

70 Pine Street

The 70 Pine Street is a skyscraper in Manhattan's financial district, New York City. The building was built between 1929 and 1932 and was initially known as the American International. The project was designed by architects Clinton & Russell and Holton & George.

The structure rises 66 floors and reaches a height of 290 meters. It was the third tallest building in New York City at its opening in 1932. 70 Pine Street was also the first building in the world to have an elevator that automatically stops on every floor.

The façade features bronze decorations with geometric patterns and plant designs, along with numerous arched windows. The interior is equally impressive, with marble floors, stone walls, and vaulted ceilings.

The building was purchased in 1979

by Citibank, which used it as its headquarters until 2015. Later, the skyscraper was converted into a luxury residential complex.

In 2008, the façade of the building was restored, while in 2016 a new atrium of 3,000 square meters was inaugurated, which preserved the original Art Deco design.

The project was born in the early 30s of the twentieth century during the Great Depression that had led to a global economic crisis. The ownership of the land, located in Manhattan's financial district, belonged to the Cities Service Company, an oil company that decided to sell the area to a group of investors led by real estate company The Red Apple Rest Corporation. The latter commissioned the project to the Japanese architect Yoshia S. Chen, who had already worked on several skyscraper projects in New York. The original design called for a 67-story building, but was later expanded to 71 to meet the growing demand for office space. The idea was funded by John J. Raskob, an American entrepreneur and philanthropist. The construction of the skyscraper began in 1930 and ended in 1932, in just 24 months.

70 Pine Street is an example of Art Deco architecture. Its façade is decorated in pink limestone with a series of towers and

spires that give the building an imposing appearance. One of the distinguishing features is its Gothic-style tower that rises on top of the building.

The construction of the skyscraper had some difficulties such as the need to develop construction techniques to allow the construction of such a tall building. The solution was to use a steel frame, a cutting-edge technology at the time. In addition, its construction was hampered by a series of workers' strikes, which delayed the work for several months.

The interior spaces of the skyscraper are divided into offices and residential apartments. The first 24 floors are dedicated entirely to the executive area, while the remaining are divided between residences and common areas. The apartments have been built since 2009 and are available in different types, from studios to four-room apartments.

70 Pine Street is currently owned by the real estate company Rose Associates, which acquired the building in 2014 and most of the interior spaces are rented to several companies. Some of the current renters include American Express bank, consulting firm McKinsey & Company, insurance company AIG and media firm Conde Nast.

It is a mixed-use building, so some parts are only accessible to residents or employees of the companies that work there. However, there are some parts that can be visited. The building's lobby, which has undergone a complete renovation, is open to the public and is an excellent example of Art Deco design from the 30s. Guests can admire the coffered ceiling and marble floors.

In addition, the 66th floor has recently been transformed into a public lounge area, called "The Terrace Club".

To visit 70 Pine Street, you can book a guided tour through the building's website or contact the front desk directly for more information.

The 19 MOST FAMOUS SKYSCRAPERS IN NEW YORK:
THE COMPLETE GUIDE

MetLife Building

The MetLife Building, also known as the Pan Am Building, is a skyscraper located at 200 Park Avenue. It was commissioned in 1958 by Pan American World Airways to be used as headquarters and terminal. However, in 1960, the Metropolitan Life Insurance Company acquired the building and used it as its headquarters until 2005.

The skyscraper, 246 meters high and with 59 floors, was completed in 1963 and was one of the first buildings in New York to have a glass façade. The modern design was inspired by the European architecture of the Bauhaus.

The original design called for a 100-story building, but due to height restrictions imposed by the New York City Master Plan, construction was reduced to 59 floors.

It was built between 1960 and 1963,

with an innovative system called "slipform", which allowed a plan to be completed every three days.

The style of the building is an example of the Modern Movement, with a steel and glass structure and a granite façade. It has a parallelepiped shape, a three-story base with "H" shaped pillars. The granite façade was made in Italy and transported by sea. The stone was chosen for its weather resistance and for its elegant and durable appearance.

The MetLife Building was built on the site of the former Grand Central Terminal. Its demolition had aroused great controversy. The construction presented several construction problems. One of the main ones was the placement of the huge steel pylons in the center of the structure. They were so large that it was necessary to demolish a church to allow the entry of building materials.

Currently, the MetLife Building is owned by investment firm Tishman Speyer, which purchased the building in 2005 for about $1.72 billion.

Renters include major companies and organizations, such as the Council on Foreign Relations, Credit Suisse, Greenberg Traurig, Hunton Andrews Kurth, Metropolitan Life Insurance Company, and WeWork.

The MetLife Building is a commercial building and is not open to the public for sightseeing. However, the lobby is accessible to the public during business hours. You can also admire the skyscraper from several nearby locations, such as Bryant Park and the Empire State Building.

The 19 MOST FAMOUS SKYSCRAPERS IN NEW YORK:
THE COMPLETE GUIDE

The Citigroup Center

The Citigroup Center is a skyscraper located at 601 Lexington Avenue, between 53rd and 54th Streets, in Manhattan. It was completed in 1977 and has a height of 279 meters. The project was commissioned by First National City Bank, which later became Citibank and eventually Citigroup.

The project was carried out by American architect Hugh Stubbins of Skidmore, Owings and Merrill (SOM) and was the first skyscraper in the United States to have a triangulation system on the roof that makes it windproof.

The architectural style of the Citigroup Center can be defined as modern and functional, with its parallelepiped-shaped structure and its steel and glass facades. A distinctive feature of the skyscraper is the large diagonal on the southwest façade that allowed to create a large atrium open to the public at the corner of 53rd Street and Lexington Avenue.

The project was developed by Hugh Stubbins & Associates, a well-known American architecture firm, and was built between 1974 and 1977 in New York City.

The design of the building was influenced by the choice of hexagonal shape, which created a number of challenges in construction. Its structure consists of a grid of steel beams that extend along the facades of the building. These beams form a sort of "X" offering greater seismic stability and allowing to eliminate the need for internal support columns.

In addition, a unique feature of the building is the large atrium that opens onto 53rd Street. It was designed to allow access to underground public transport and provided space for the installation of a sculpture by Alexander Calder called "Harrison's Arc".

It also presented a challenge regarding its location and the need to build the building above the metro station. To do so, the building was raised on 114 columns, strategically positioned to avoid interfering with the area below. As for the materials used, the structure of the building is made of steel and the outer casing is made of glass.

During the construction of the Citigroup Center, there were several construction problems that required major repairs.

The Citigroup Center suffered problems during its construction when it was discovered that the junctions of the beams were too weak and could cause them to collapse in case of too strong winds. To solve this problem, four large buttresses were added to the base. The building was anchored and all the joints of the beams were replaced. This work was completed in 1978, two years after the opening of the complex. These interventions cost about 50 million dollars.

The Citigroup Center was designed to be used as the headquarters of the bank of the same name. The interior spaces have been designed to meet the specific needs of the company, but over time have been modified to adapt to the demands of the new owners.

Now, the Citigroup Center is owned by Boston Properties. Currently, the building is mainly leased by Citigroup, the global finance company, which is based in the tower and occupies a large part of the interior spaces. Other renters include several financial, legal and real estate services firms.

The skyscraper is not open to the

public in the traditional way, as access to the interior is limited to employees of companies based there and authorized visitors. However, you can join the tours of the Open House New York, a tour operator that organizes free visits to buildings and sites of architectural interest throughout New York City.

The 19 MOST FAMOUS SKYSCRAPERS IN NEW YORK:
THE COMPLETE GUIDE

30 Hudson Yards

The 30 Hudson Yards is a skyscraper located in the Hudson Yards building complex in Manhattan. It is 387 meters high and features a modern design characterized by a prismatic shape that narrows upwards, culminating in a pointed top. The structure is clad in glass and stainless steel that reflects the surrounding environment.

The tower has been designed to be eco-sustainable, with the aim of achieving LEED Gold certification. Among the features, the skyscraper features a rainwater recovery system for irrigation and a water cooler that comes directly from the Hudson River and reduces energy consumption.

Inside there are offices, restaurants and a panoramic observatory, called "The Edge" which offers a breathtaking view of the city.

The design of the building was developed by Kohn Pedersen Fox Associates, a New York-based architecture firm, on behalf of Related Companies and Oxford Properties Group. The original idea was to build a building that would be an icon of the new Hudson Yards neighborhood, and that would offer space for offices and the public. The design of the skyscraper was conceived to evoke the shape of a diamond.

The design is characterized by its clean lines that recall the shapes of the sails of a ship. The building consists of a square base that extends upwards, with two side protrusions that converge at the top, creating a sort of arch. The external façade is entirely covered in glass.

The stylistic choices are focused on the creation of modern and functional spaces, with a strong focus on environmental sustainability. For this reason, 30 Hudson Yards was designed to be an eco-friendly building, equipped with many cutting-edge technologies.

As for the materials used, the building was made of steel, concrete and glass, while the external façade is clad with anodized aluminum panels that give it a clean and modern look.

The project involved a number of technical and architectural challenges, particularly due to the location of the site, previously used as a railway station. To cope with this problem, engineers designed a huge reinforced concrete platform to cover the railway tracks below.

The upper floors house the panoramic observatory "The Edge". The elevators leading to the terrace are considered the fastest in the U.S.A.

The building is owned by Related Companies and Oxford Properties Group. Designed as an office skyscraper, it is home to numerous firms, including consulting firm McKinsey & Company, consulting firm KKR, private equity firm Blackstone Group, investment firm PointState Capital and investment management firm D1 Capital Partners. In addition, the building is also the headquarters of WarnerMedia.

Some public areas within the Hudson Yards complex, such as the art and design store "Snark Park", the large shopping center and the panoramic terrace, are accessible to visitors.

Time Warner Center

The Time Warner Center is a complex of skyscrapers located near Columbus Circle. It consists of two twin 55-story buildings, which are located across from Central Park. Its construction began in 2000 and ended in 2003.

The project was developed by a team of architects led by Skidmore, Owings & Merrill (SOM) and interior designer David Rockwell.

The building was conceived as a multifunctional complex that was supposed to house a variety of commercial, cultural and residential activities. Its realization was made possible thanks to the partnership between the Time Warner Group and the real estate company The Related Companies. The site was previously occupied by the New York Coliseum demolished in 2000.

The architects tried to combine

modern design elements with references to the architectural tradition of the city. The main buildings are is 229 meters high.

The architectural style is characterized by a modern and bold design, with a glass and steel façade. The building, consisting of two twin towers, has a central base that houses the Time Warner Center Mall, a luxurious shopping mall with numerous shops, restaurants, and a multiplex cinema. The lobby is a work of art by design, with marble floors and ceilings up to 10 meters high.

The complex was the first in the United States to achieve LEED Silver certification for energy efficiency and environmental sustainability.

During its construction, some technical and structural problems emerged. One of the main ones was the proximity of the construction site to the subway lines. In addition, problems were found related to the waterproofing of the foundations and water infiltration, which required repairs to ensure their structural safety.

The site had previously been used as a coal depot and therefore issues related to land reclamation and removal of contaminated materials had to be addressed.

The Time Warner Center is divided

into two towers, each of which has its own entrance. The north is used for residential use, the south is home to the offices of Time Warner Inc. as well as the luxury hotel Mandarin Oriental.

Inside there are also many commercial activities: high fashion shops, restaurants and a fitness center.

The Time Warner Center was acquired by Related Companies in 2014 for approximately $1.3 billion. It is currently operated by Time Warner Center Management LLC, a joint venture between Related Companies and Oxford Properties Group. Renters include companies such as Time Warner Inc., Citigroup and Warner Music Group.

In addition, the Time Warner Center is home to some of the city's most renowned restaurants, including Per Se, Masa, and Bouchon Bakery.

The structure is open to the public but to access it you must have a valid reason, such as an appointment with a company that is based there, or a reservation in one of the restaurants or shops within the structure. It is not possible to visit the towers only for tourist reasons or curiosity.

Spruce Street – Beekman Tower

The Spruce Street - Beekman Tower, is a skyscraper located in Lower Manhattan. Designed by architect Frank Gehry, it was completed in 2011 and is considered one of New York's most iconic skyscrapers.

It is located at the intersection of William Street and Spruce Street, near New York City Hall and Brooklyn Bridge. With 265 meters high and its 76 floors, it is the tallest building in Lower Manhattan south of the World Trade Center.

The style of the building is strongly influenced by the work of architect Frank Gehry. The Beekman has an undulating façade composed of curved glass windows that create an effect of movement and fluidity. Curves are created by a system of steel beams and pillars, which also provide structural strength.

The project was commissioned by the real estate company Forest City Ratner

Companies in 2003. The idea was to create a large building that would be able to revive the Lower Manhattan area after the events of September 11, 2001.

One of the main challenges for Gehry was to create a skyscraper that would be able to integrate into the surrounding urban context characterized by historic buildings from different eras. He decided to use a mix of materials for the façade of the building, which gives it a dynamic and modern look.

The project was approved in 2006 and construction began in 2007, but was slowed down by the 2008 financial crisis. However, work resumed in 2009 and the building was completed in 2011. The total cost was about $875 million.

The architectural style is defined as "deconstructivist", as it presents a fragmented and asymmetrical aesthetic, with curved and inclined surfaces. The architect's choices are also reflected in the internal structure, where the corridors are curved and the walls are sloping, creating a unique spatial experience for those who live there.

As for the materials, the building has a steel and concrete structure, while the interior finishes are made of high quality materials such as marble, granite and precious wood.

The exterior is characterized by the presence of a series of "folds" that give the skyscraper a sculpted appearance.

The project was subject to several implementation problems. One of the main obstacles was the presence of the metro crossing the site. To overcome this difficulty, inclined foundation piles were made.

The owner of the building is Silverstein Properties, a real estate company that manages buildings around the world.

The Beekman Tower is not open to the public for sightseeing or sightseeing. However, interested parties may consider registering for a public event hosted in the building, such as concerts or art exhibitions.

The 19 MOST FAMOUS SKYSCRAPERS IN NEW YORK:
THE COMPLETE GUIDE

The Helmsley Building

The Helmsley Building, also known as the New York Central Building, is a building located at 230 Park Avenue, in the heart of Manhattan's business district. Built in 1929, it was designed by architect Warren & Wetmore, who also designed the famous Grand Central Terminal station, located just a few blocks away.

The building is spread over 35 floors and is 169 meters high, making it one of the tallest skyscrapers of the Art Deco period. Its white stone façade is characterized by sculptural decorations and elaborate details.

The property was restored in the 90s to restore its original appearance, including the green copper domed building that was renovated in 2012. Inside there is also a large shopping arcade, which houses several shops and restaurants.

The Helmsley Building was listed on the National Register of Historic Places in 1987.

The project originated in the second half of the '20s, when real estate magnate William H. Reynolds commissioned the construction of a new skyscraper on New York's Park Avenue.

Construction began in 1928, but slowed down due to the Great Depression of the 30s. However, work resumed when real estate developer Harry Helmsley bought the building and completed it with a number of modifications and improvements. In particular, Helmsley, had a new technical plan built and added decorative elements to the façade, such as large Roman numeral clocks.

The Helmsley Building was designed in the Beaux-Arts style, very popular in America at the beginning of the twentieth century. The design was influenced by the nearby Grand Central Terminal, completed only a few years earlier.

The building was designed to house offices and commercial spaces. The interiors feature a functional design, with bright and open spaces.

The ground floor is dedicated to the lobby with a large reception area for visitors and a reception desk. There are commercial spaces a restaurant and a coffee shop.

The upper floors are dedicated to offices, are divided into open and private spaces. The former are used to house the employees of the companies based in the building, while the private spaces are intended for meeting rooms, executive offices and secretaries.

The Helmsley Building is owned by the investment firm Empire State Realty Trust. The tenants of the building include several companies and organizations, including financial services firm Wells Fargo, consulting firm McKinsey & Company, National Football League (NFL), National Hockey League (NHL).

It is a mainly office building and is not open to the public for sightseeing. However, there are some exceptions where you can visit it. For example, the lobby occasionally hosts public art exhibitions, and there are also special events held in the lobby, such as concerts and dance performances. In addition, some of the shops and restaurants inside the building are open and accessible.

As for the guided tours, it is possible that some are organized by tourism companies specialized in architectural visits, but it is necessary to contact them directly for information on any programs.

The 19 MOST FAMOUS SKYSCRAPERS IN NEW YORK:
THE COMPLETE GUIDE

Central Park Tower

The Central Park Tower is one of the tallest skyscrapers in the world and is located at 225 West 57th Street, in the heart of Midtown Manhattan.

It is 472 meters high, has 98 floors, and was completed in 2019. It contains 179 luxury residential units, a hotel and offices.

The building has a pointed shape that narrows upwards, with a steel frame and a glass façade offering panoramic views.

The Central Park Tower uses state-of-the-art technology to ensure environmental sustainability and energy efficiency. It is equipped with a controlled airflow ventilation system, an efficient lighting system, a rainwater collection tank and a waste recycling system.

The Central Park Tower project, also known as Nordstrom Tower, was announced in 2012 by Extell Development Company, a

New York City real estate company.

The building was designed by architect Adrian Smith, known for designing Dubai's Burj Khalifa, and Gordon Gill's architectural firm. The design has undergone numerous changes over the years, especially with regard to the height of the building. Initially, the tower was supposed to reach a height of 541 meters but the first sketches were rejected due to safety concerns.

In 2014, real estate company JDS Development Group joined the project as a development partner. In 2015, it was announced the creation of a wing of the building that houses the logistics space of the Nordstrom chain, from which the skyscraper got the unofficial name of "Nordstrom Tower".

After years of planning and construction, the Central Park Tower opened in 2020.

The skyscraper has a modern and innovative design, with geometric and sinuous lines that distinguish it from other buildings. The tower is characterized by a glass shell structure and a series of vertical cuts on the façade that create a dynamic and refined texture. Its slender shape, with a triangular ledge at the top, makes it one of the most iconic buildings on the New York cityscape.

Its construction presented several challenges. One of the biggest problems was managing the flow of traffic around the construction site. The street at West 57th Street had to be closed to traffic to ensure the safety of workers and pedestrians, which created significant congestion problems. In addition, the site's proximity to Central Park made construction logistics even more complicated, as it was necessary to coordinate the delivery of materials and the transit of workers in an area with a high population density. The fact that the Central Park Tower was designed to be one of the tallest skyscrapers in the world presented a number of bureaucratic problems regarding the concessions to be obtained. Local authorities had to carefully examine the project to ensure it complied with all safety regulations.

The Central Park Tower is divided into 179 residential units, with a maximum of three units per floor. The residences range from the 63 square meter studio up to the 1034 square meter triplex penthouse.

Access to the building is guaranteed by a large double-height entrance hall that leads to a series of high-speed elevators.

Due to the private nature of the building, you cannot visit it as freely as you would with a tourist attraction. However, it is possible to book guided tours through agencies that specialize in visits to iconic buildings in New York.

Flat Iron Building

The Flatiron Building is a historic building in New York City located at 175 Fifth Avenue, at the intersection of Broadway and 22nd Street. It is one of the most iconic skyscrapers in the city and the world, despite not being very tall compared to its modern "neighbors".

The building was designed by architect Daniel Burnham in 1901 and completed in 1902. It is 87 meters high. It has a steel structure, covered in white terracotta. It features an unusual triangular design due to the irregularity of the wedge-shaped area in which it is located.

Its design was inspired by the shape of an iron case, with the long side oriented towards the main road. This unusual design required the use of advanced construction techniques for the time.

The building was one of the first skyscrapers in New York and one of the first to use elevators. It was also one of the first buildings to be equipped with electric central heating, air conditioning and a fire alarm system.

The Flatiron Building was the subject of some controversy during its construction. Some people were concerned that the building would not be able to withstand the strong gusts of wind occurring in the area. However, the building was designed to withstand all the extreme weather conditions that occur in Manhattan.

The idea of building the Flatiron Building was born from the need to make the best use of a triangular space created at the intersection of Fifth Avenue and Broadway, where the latter obliquely cuts the rectangle of the Manhattan street grid. The investment firm Fuller Company, which owned the land, wanted to build a tall, prestigious building that would stand out from other skyscrapers of the time, and entrusted the task to Burnham.

The architect was inspired by the solutions used in European constructions, in particular, the large iron and glass buildings of France, where he himself had worked on the construction of the building of the Universal Exhibition of 1889. The design involved a steel structure and an isosceles trapezoid shape, with a wide base that gradually narrowed. Its design represented a real revolution in the architecture of skyscrapers of the time.

Today it is considered one of the symbols of New York and has been listed on the National Register of Historic Places of the United States. Its peculiar shape and style make it one of the most photographed and admired buildings in the city.

The exterior cladding of the building is in terracotta, with cast iron details. The facades have an elaborate design, with a large number of windows, decorations and details. The main façade is characterized by a large arch that embraces the entrance.

The ground floor is occupied by a few shops, including Starbucks, a bike shop and a book store. It mainly houses offices, which have been flexibly divided.

The twenty-third floor, which was originally used as the building's owner's apartment, has been converted into a modern event space, with large windows offering panoramic views. In the past, the Flatiron Building has also housed some art galleries and artists' studios.

The palace houses a variety of companies and organizations, including offices, law firms, advertising agencies, art galleries, and restaurants. Major tenants include the National Museum of Mathematics, film production company Sony Pictures Classics, and advertising agency R/GA.

Although the Flatiron Building is a historic building, it is not open to the public for sightseeing. However, you can admire its exterior architecture by strolling around or sitting in one of the many cafes or restaurants nearby. In addition, there are guided tours that include a short stop at the Flatiron Building.

Printed in Great Britain
by Amazon